New York

New York
Gateway to America

John Bowman

Bison Books

First published in 1985 by
Bison Books Ltd
176 Old Brompton Road
London SW5
England

ISBN 0 86124 239 4

Printed in Holland

Page 1 To many people, the Statue of Liberty
symbolizes the city of New York.
Page 2 A magical view of the Manhattan
skyline at night, seen from the Queens side of
the East River.
Bathed in golden sunlight, the Statue of
Liberty continues to greet one and all to this
gateway to the New World.

Acknowledgements

The author and publisher would like to thank the following people
who have helped in the preparation of this book: Richard and
Sonja Glassman who designed it; Elizabeth Miles Montgomery
who edited it; Mary Raho who did the picture research.

Picture credits

Bart Barlow 2-3, 6, 12, 13 bottom, 16, 18 bottom, 19 top, 20, 26
top, 32, 33 top, 39 top, 43 top right and bottom left,
44-45, 46-47, 48 top and bottom, 50-51, 53 top, 56
bottom right, 57, 62 top, 64 top and bottom, 69 top,
70 left, 74-75, 79 right, 81, 88-89, 89 middle, 94 left
bottom.
John Calabrese 26 bottom, 27 bottom, 55 left, 70-71 bottom, 86
right top, 94 top.
FPG/International 1 (P Gridley); 4-5 (D Hallinan); 8-9 (P Gridley);
10-11 (D Hallinan); 11 (T Sanderling); 13 (L
Goldman); 14-15 (A and A Graphics); 17 left (E
Croper), right (J Hamel); 18 (P Gridley); 19
right (Alexas Urba); 21 top (Co Rentmeesters),
bottom left (K Reinhard), bottom right (Flash
Pictures Inc); 23 (Larsen Photographs); 25 (J L
Bergmann); 27 top (A Giampiccolo), right
(Marmel Studios); 28 (L Cherney); 29 top (A L
Goldman), bottom left (T Qing), bottom right (J
Hamel); 30-31 (B March); 34 top (W
Choroszewski), bottom left (Granada Studios),
bottom right (N Ney); 35 (J Ciganovic); 36-37 (F
Lazi); 38 (L Cherney); 40 (M Tamborino); 40-41
(B March); 41 (Marmel Studios); 42 bottom left
(Chicago Stock Finders), right (Co
Rentmeesters); 43 top left (Co Rentmeesters),
bottom left (Marmel Studios), bottom right (J
Zalon); 47 (D Bartruff); 49 (B Byers); 52-53 (R
Laird); 54 (D Bartruff); 55 top right (P
Weschler), bottom right (Naison Agency); 56 top
(P Gridley), bottom left (D Hallinan); 58-59 (K
Rubin); 60-61 (G Geller); 61 top (J Baker); 62
bottom (Camera Work); 63 top (J Hamel),
bottom (W Choroszewski); 64 (Camera
Graphics); 66-67 (Wilson Photo); 68-69
(Newsworld Communications); 70-71 top (J
Zalon), center (M Dominguez); 71 top right (J
Wegewiser), bottom right (L Cherney); 72 top
left (C Rubin); 72-23 top (W Choroszewski),
bottom (R Laird); 73 top right (Pastner); 76-77
(S Hopkins); 77 (R Rossi); 78 left (L Bradley),
top right (L Marshall); 79 top left (Co
Rentmeesters); 82-83 (L Bradley); 84-85 (L
Bradley); 85 top (B March); 86 left (A
Giampiccolo), bottom right (M Stein); 87
(Zimmerman); 92-93 (M Dominguez); 93 top (M
Tamborino); 94 bottom right (J Schorr); 95 top
(Marmel Studios), bottom (J Hamel); 96
(Llewellyn).
Eric Marcusson 19 left, 24-25, 80, 89 top.
Pamela Marcusson 40 top right, 72 bottom left.
Museum of the City of New York 73 bottom.
New York Racing Association 89 bottom.
The Pierpont Morgan Library 42 top.
Roger Morris-Jumel Mansion 78-79.

Contents

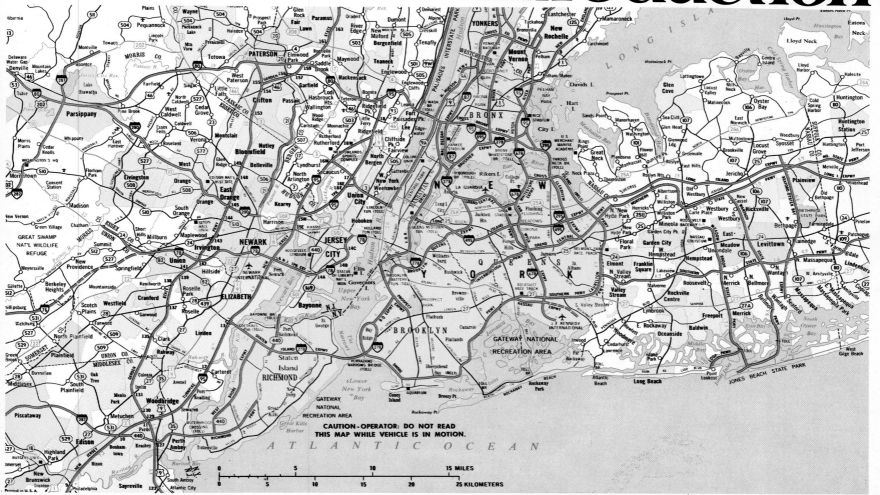

CAUTION - OPERATOR: DO NOT READ
THIS MAP WHILE VEHICLE IS IN MOTION.

Is there any city in the world today quite like New York City? Quite so exciting, so stimulating, so infused with a dynamic and contemporary spirit? New Yorkers themselves are not the only people who might make this claim, for people from all over the world can be heard saying this—and being drawn to the unique city to visit or to settle. Yet where does this special spirit of New York come from?

It does not come especially from its size, for there are increasing numbers of more populous cities; already Shanghai, Mexico City, Tokyo, and Peking are larger. But all these cities share another quality besides being bigger than New York: they are all relatively homogeneous. Each has a population of more or less the same ethnic–national origin and more or less the same histories and traditions and lifestyles. New York City's distinguishing characteristic—in every sphere, in every dimension—is its diversity, the constant and pervasive mixture of peoples and styles, whether in architecture, foods, holidays or urban environments. New York City, in a word, is cosmopolitan.

It should come as no surprise that a city as large and cosmopolitan as New York evokes different responses from different people. Big cities have always done so, and it is also a tradition to brand such cities as wicked and decadent. Babylon remains synonymous with this image of the cosmopolitan city; ancient Rome took over that image; Paris and London assumed the role in modern times; now New York inherits the scarlet mantle. If non–New Yorkers want to think of the city in this way, that is their perogative, but they should know that New Yorkers do not necessarily experience their city this way. They live in a different city, one that is conveyed in all its various dimensions in the photographs of this volume.

Many visitors to New York are attracted and dazzled by its modernity—the great glittering skyscrapers that continue to evolve new styles, the museums and galleries with the latest schools of art, the swankiest nightspots, all the most recent fashions and fads. But New Yorkers also know another city, an older, more mellow city, not only in the sense of New York's colorful past, reflected in its historical buildings, but in the persistence of traditional ways of living. Most New Yorkers still walk to the store, for instance, and that store is not apt to be a gigantic supermarket in a mall.

For just as many non-New Yorkers are amazed at—or appalled by—the sheer size of the city, they fail to realize that most New Yorkers do not think of themselves as living in that entire city. When they read about crime or violence in some other borough or section of town, they might as well be reading about events in a different city. For although a New Yorker may commute to another borough or area to work, he *lives* in only one neighborhood. He patronizes the shops and services within a few blocks, chats on the street with neighbors and shopkeepers and often works with block associations or similar community groups. He occupies one of the thousands of niches that comprise the vast city.

If this more mellow, traditional, conventional New York City isn't always featured in travelers' tales and photographs, it may be because it is not so dramatic as the skyscrapers. But both the mellow and the dramatic, the neighborhoods and the skyscrapers, are part of the true New York. And that New York is captured here.

Opposite When New Yorkers celebrate the Fourth of July with fireworks over the Hudson River and the illuminated towers of Midtown, their city of metal and stone becomes one of air and light.

The World Trade Center towers over the financial district at the tip of Manhattan.

The Harbor

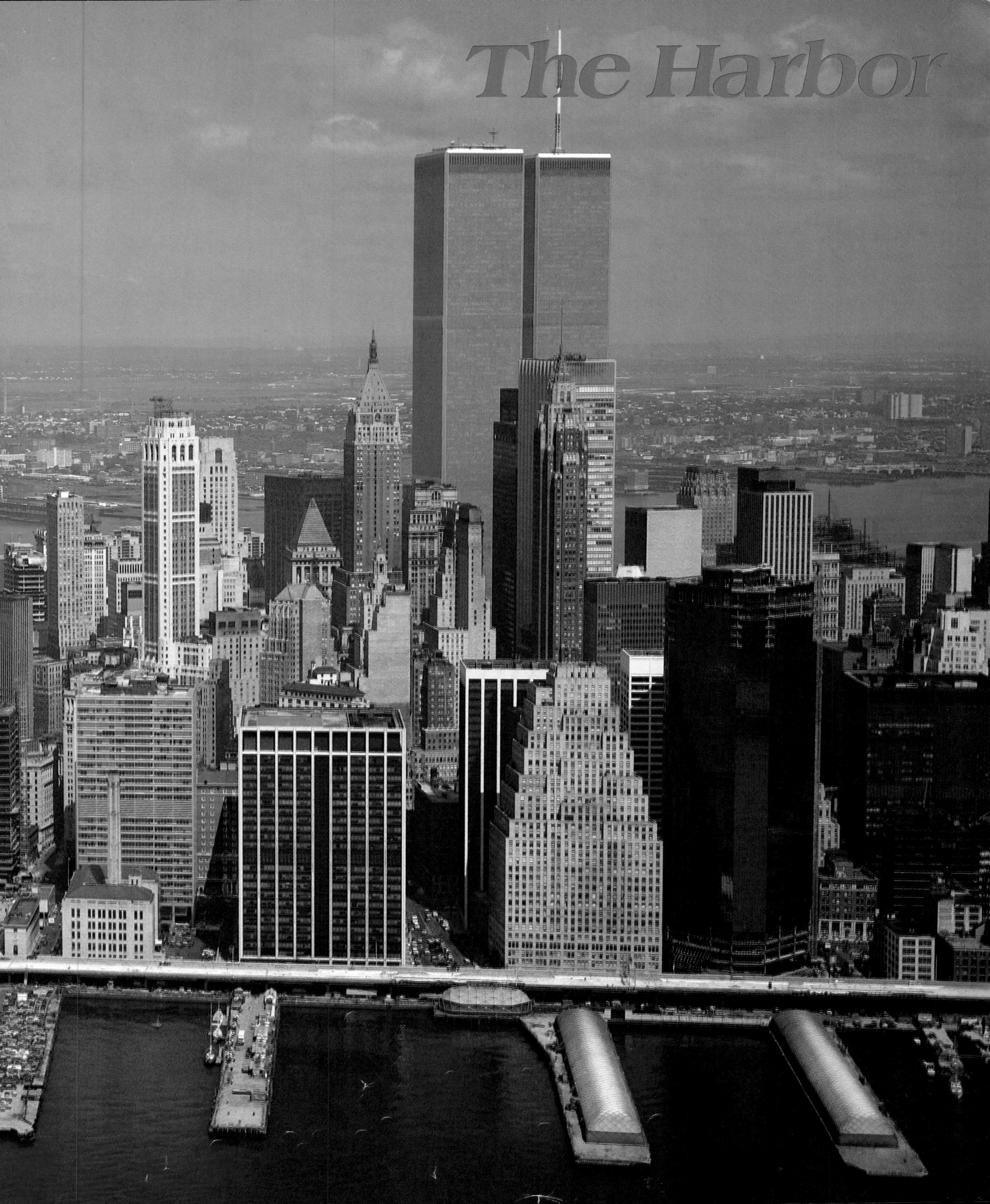

The Harbor

From the arrival of Henry Hudson and the first Dutch colonists in the early seventeenth century through the millions of Old World immigrants to the latest jet-plane passengers, the first view of New York City for most arrivals is the tip of Lower Manhattan. For New York City is, above all else, a seaport—indeed, an island city—and much of its life has traditionally centered on the buildings and activities that grew up around the tip of Manhattan.

Today, the port of New York is still one of the busiest in the world, even though its energy level may no longer be registered solely by the tonnage of merchant, passenger, or military ships. As always, the harbor of New York City throbs with life in a way that is both functional and symbolic. For many people of the world, for instance, the Statue of Liberty, which stands just off Lower Manhattan, remains the ideal symbol of the United States of America. And on nearby Ellis Island was located the actual processing center for millions of immigrants from the Old World.

But for both New Yorkers and many others, whether one-time visitors or permanent residents, the spirit of New York City is perhaps best symbolized by the dramatic skyline of Lower Manhattan. From the earliest years of the twentieth century, the Manhattan skyline has made an impact on all who see it for the first time: it is reported that the German film director Fritz Lang, upon approaching New York City by ship in the 1920s, was inspired to make his futuristic-Utopian classic, *Metropolis*, and this skyline can still evoke an emotional response when pictured in anything from a travel poster to a Hollywood film.

In recent years, there has been yet another dimension added to the life of Lower Manhattan and its surrounding waters: increasing numbers of new buildings are going up on the tip of Manhattan and drawing more New Yorkers than ever to work and live there. The World Trade Center is the best known of these recent additions, but many other new skyscrapers are adding to the functional and aesthetic dimensions of this part of New York City. Henry Hudson might not recognize the skyline, but he would certainly know that he had arrived at someplace special.

Above A fireboat of the New York City Fire Department docked off Lower Manhattan, ready to protect the miles of harbor and piers.
Left The twin towers of the World Trade Center—at 1350 feet, the second highest building in the world—rise above the Hudson River and the New York financial district. The hotel below the towers is part of the ambitious Battery Park City project.

Far left Formally named 'Statue of Liberty Enlightening the World,' this grand monument has been greeting all who arrive in New York since her unveiling on 28 October 1886. Originally conceived in 1865 by the French to commemorate the Franco-American alliance in the American Revolution, the statue was designed by Frederic-August Bertholdi (who used his mother as the model).

Left top The old South Brooklyn Ferry Pier off Battery Park at the tip of Manhattan is the home port for the fireboats that protect the great harbor of New York.

Left bottom In preparation of the 100th anniversary of the dedication, the Statue of Liberty underwent a total renovation in the 1980s that required the erection of a mammoth scaffolding. The surface of the statue is made up of 300 hammered copper plates, on a framework created by Gustave Eiffel, the designer of the Eiffel Tower.

Right One of the famed Staten Island ferries that ply between Manhattan and Staten Island day and night. In addition to the many Staten Island residents who commute to Manhattan in this delightful manner, the 25 million annual passengers include tourists from all over the world who find the ferry ride an ideal way to view New York and the harbor.

Below Now a National Park, the US Immigration Station on Ellis Island was built in 1898; some 12 million immigrants passed through before it closed in 1954.

The graceful Federal building that is New
York City Hall was completed in 1811

Wall Street and City Hall

Wall Street and City Hall

To many out−of−towners, New York City is Manhattan, and Manhattan is itself often defined by midtown sights and excitements. But there are many other distinct parts to Manhattan, areas where hundreds of thousands of New Yorkers work or live or both. One of these areas, primarily a place to work, is the southernmost part of Manhattan known as 'downtown,' which includes many government buildings as well as the financial district that is universally known as Wall Street.

This downtown area was the site of the original Dutch settlement in the seventeenth century, and in 1653 Governor Peter Stuyvesant called for the construction of a wall of planks stretching from the Hudson to the East River. The English took over Nieuw Amsterdam in 1664, and removed the wall in 1699; it was replaced by a street, on one corner of which the English built their own city hall, the present site of the Federal Hall National Museum. In the early nineteenth century a new city hall was erected on a site somewhat to the north of Wall Street.

The long association of Wall Street with stocks and finance began in 1792 when 24 brokers assembled at a buttonwood tree on the corner of Wall and Williams Streets and established the forerunner of the New York Stock Exchange. This part of Manhattan remained the center of life throughout the eighteenth century, and inevitably both government and commercial institutions settled here. The harbor area also flourished—as witnessed by the fine buildings that are now part the South Street Seaport Museum.

But New York was constantly expanding and by the mid-nineteenth century there were over 50,000 people living across the East River in Brooklyn. From the earliest times, ferry boats had provided the sole link with Manhattan, but after the Civil War some Brooklynites agreed that a bridge would be necessary if Brooklyn was to share fully in the life of New York. Construction began in 1870, and although its designer, John A Roebling, died at the outset—from infection due to a foot crushed by a ferryboat—his son, Washington, saw it through to completion in 1883.

Opposite The Brooklyn Bridge was built between 1869-1883 by the Roeblings, father and son. It is generally regarded as one of the finest examples of the marriage of technology and esthetics.
Left Trinity Church, completed in 1846, was designed by Richard Upjohn. Its cemetary contains the tombs of such revolutionary notables as Alexander Hamilton.
Above Sidewalk vendors are still a fixture of life in New York.

Opposite top New York's financial district as seen from the Port of Brooklyn where ships of all types and sizes may be found.

Opposite bottom This row of buildings, now part of the South Street Seaport Museum, was built about 1800.

Top The old Fulton Fish Market, now incorporated into the South Street Seaport, is filled with exotic food shops and restaurants.

Left The gambrel-roofed farmhouse at 2 White Street, built about 1780 now houses a barbershop, a typical reuse of an old building.

Above Fresh fish were delivered right off the boats and sold daily at the Fulton Fish Market, now relocated in the Bronx.

19

Opposite Ticker-tape parades up Broadway are the traditional New York way of greeting celebrities. Here the paper flutters down in front of the Woolworth building, built in 1913 and considered one of New York's first skyscrapers.

Above A typical scene at the New York Stock exchange where millions of shares in major American companies are bought and sold each day.

Left The statue of George Washington stands on the steps of the former US Custom House, erected in 1842 on the site of the Federal Hall, where Washington took the oath as President in 1789.

Below Fraunces Tavern has been just that ever since 1762, when Samuel Fraunces opened for business. It was here that Washington said farewell to his officers in 1783.

The many Chinese who live in New York's Chinatown celebrate their New Year with a dragon, symbolizing the force of Nature.

The Lower East Side

All of America is, of course, a land composed of immigrants, but nowhere is this still more evident than in the section of Manhattan known as the Lower East Side. Fourteenth Street forms its northern boundary, the East River its eastern, the Brooklyn Bridge its southern, while its western boundary winds up along the edge of Chinatown and Little Italy to Second or Third Avenues, which rejoin 14th Street. But the Lower East Side has another, more localized meaning, and that is the predominantly Jewish sections and way of life that took root in a somewhat more restricted portion of this area.

The reasons why particular groups of immigrants settled precisely where they did—the Italians in what would become Little Italy, the Chinese in what was to be Chinatown, the Jews in what became their Lower East Side—are lost in the mists of time and may have little more to do than with the chance settling down of the first of their numbers off the boats. Very quickly though, they came to feel that life would be easier for all concerned if they stayed among their own kind. And so there grew up by the end of the nineteenth century these particular communities, with their own shops, services, restaurants, signs and newspapers, houses of worship—everything that would make these people feel more 'at home' in this strange new city.

Not all these communities have remained stable or homogeneous, although Chinatown has if anything grown larger and stronger in recent years, due largely to an influx of immigrants from Hong Kong. Little Italy's residents multiplied and prospered and most of the second and later generations of Italian–Americans have moved out; but there are still many who have remained to keep alive their traditions. As for the Lower East Side of the Jews who were crowded there in the last decade of the nineteenth century and first decades of the twentieth century, that has undergone the greatest change in its ethnic composition: many Puerto Ricans and Dominicans now live there—alas, many in the same tenements that would have been regarded as marginal by their original Jewish occupants decades ago—but there are also many Slavic groups, Ukrainians and Poles in particular, some Black–Americans, and more recent groups such as Filipinos. One thing remains constant: the Lower East Side's own lively and nurturing atmosphere.

Left Many of the ethnic, national and religious communities of New York hold traditional annual festivals. One of the liveliest and best attended of these is that of San Gennaro, held in Little Italy.
Above Orchard Street on the Lower East Side is lined with shops that remain open on Sunday, attracting customers from all over looking for bargains.

Above and below Tenement apartments that were built in the nineteenth and early twentieth centuries have since been required to add unsightly fire escapes, but New Yorkers brighten up these facades with paint and flowers.

Opposite top New Yorkers often create their own private retreats, and one favorite is a garden on any available rooftop, such as this one in the East Village.

Opposite bottom This brightly painted building on the Lower East Side is typical of the way New Yorkers have found to enliven their environment.

Right One of the more spectacular developments on the street of recent years has been the appearance of monumental wall paintings on otherwise unused walls. This one was painted on the exposed corner of a building on Houston Street.

Opposite The clothing displayed outside a shop on Orchard Street is one of the main attractions for those who come down to the Lower East Side, looking for bargains and a bit of local color.

Below New York City's Chinatown, the second largest in the United States, is famous for its restaurants.

Above The annual street festivals, sponsored by the Italian-American community of Little Italy, feature games of chance and illuminated decorations, as well as religious observances.

Below The Italian-Americans of Little Italy continue to play the game of *bocce*, much like the game of bowls, or lawn bowling.

Washington Square Park, with a typical gathering around the central fountain; at the north side is the Memorial Arch.

Greenwich Village
and
Washington Square

Greenwich Village and Washington Square

Great cities are made up of exciting buildings and dynamic people and vibrant streetlife, but it is also true that great cities have occasional breathing spaces, clearings where everything and everyone can take at least a moment's rest. One of the best known and best loved of these in New York City is Washington Square Park, often regarded as the spiritual, if not geographic, heart of Greenwich Village, which itself is regarded as the bohemian, if not eccentric, heart of the city.

Greenwich Village, in fact, lies almost entirely west and north of Washington Square Park; its name stems from the English colonists who first settled here at the end of the seventeenth century and who named it after the town then outside of London. Throughout the eighteenth century it remained a relatively isolated village where prosperous colonists sought a retreat from the hustle and bustle of the 'city' in lower Manhattan. Greenwich Village grew rapidly in the 1790s and early 1800s when many New Yorkers fled there from a series of epidemics ravaging more populous areas. By the time the village came to be incorporated into the governmental and planning structures of New York City, its irregular streets were so settled with residential and commercial buildings that it had to be exempted from the grid plan of streets being laid down elsewhere.

So it was that from the outset Greenwich Village stood apart as something different from the rest of the city, and it continues to maintain this sense of itself to this day. Writers and artists have long chosen to live in the more humanly proportioned buildings of Greenwich Village, restaurants and shops have deliberately tried to maintain this more personal and cozy atmosphere, and young people

and out-of-towners have followed to seek out and support the eccentricities of the Village.

There had long been a marshland on the eastern edge of the village; in 1789, it was used as a potters field, or burial place for the poor and nameless. This site was also used for a hanging gallows. Then in the 1820s it was turned into a public park and parade ground for military exercises, and from that time on it became a magnet for fine houses—survivors of which still line the northern edge of the park. In 1876, a wooden arch was erected to commemorate the nation's centenary, and in 1889 this was replaced by the great stone Memorial Arch, now commemorating the centennial of Washington's taking the oath as the nation's first President. And from that time, the arch, the square, and Greenwich Village continued to be a focal point for many of the city's celebratory impulses.

Opposite A winter's day along the north side of Washington Square. The fine Greek Revival or Federal-style houses that face the square date from the 1830s. Often threatened by builders, at least their facades are unchanged since the nineteenth century.
Above This is 'The Row,' the famed line of houses along the north side of Washington Square. Now owned by New York University, they once housed prominent families, as well as such writers and artists as Edith Wharton, Henry James and Edward Hopper.

Left A typical Greenwich Village street corner features small restaurants, well-known for their cuisine and ambience. The sidewalk tables are popular throughout the warmer months with tourists and villagers alike.
Below left Although Washington Square Park is only 10 acres in size and under constant pressure from buildings, traffic and crowds, there are still graceful wooded paths within its limits.
Below One of the less-known attractions of Greenwich Village in the autumn is the annual celebration at Halloween, when scores of children and adults dress up in elaborate costumes to parade through the area, while thousands of spectators come to watch.
Opposite Washington Square Park offers diversions to people of various tastes. One of the favorites are the chess tables provided by the city, at the southwest corner of the park, where players of all ranks and ages are apt to brood over games at any hour of the day or night.

The skyscrapers of midtown Manhattan—
one of the most extraordinary vistas in the
world.

Midtown

It is understandable that to many people, especially out—of—towners, Midtown Manhattan has taken on the image of all that is most exciting (and most intimidating) about New York City. For here are all the elements that have always distinguished the great metropolises of history, here New York City earns its sobriquet, 'Baghdad on the Subway.'

It was not always so. The earliest center of life in New York City was at the lowest tip of Manhattan, but gradually the colonists moved northward up Manhattan Island. Even as late as the 1890s, 14th Street—then considered the southern border of Midtown—was still quite fashionable. There were four residential squares—Stuyvesant, Union, Gramercy, and Madison—that were regarded as suitably elegant, and none of these extended above 26th Street. The Astors, undisputed arbiters of high society in New York, still lived at 34th Street until the early 1890s.

But the drive northward up the spine of Manhattan was as inevitable and inexorable as the American drive to the West, and often as not for the same motive: to obtain cheaper land for less crowded living and more prosperous enterprises. So the fashionable people and enterprises moved steadily northward, up Fifth Avenue, Madison Avenue, Park Avenue. Indeed, in our own time, the balance has tilted, and commercial and corporate enterprises have made real estate in Midtown so expensive that only the very rich can afford to live there.

Today, 'Midtown' is as much a state of mind as a geographic area. The boundaries extend from about 26th Street to Central Park, and east to west from about Third to Eighth Avenues. There are many New Yorkers, even Manhattanites, who can go years without ever feeling the need to 'go Midtown.' But the glittering skyscrapers, the museums and churches, the chic stores and apartments, the bustling streets and theaters comprise Midtown Manhattan to the millions of people whose fast-paced footsteps echo the heartbeat of the city itself.

Left One of the two marble lions, known as Patience and Fortitude, that guard the magnificent entrance of the central branch of the New York Public Library on Fifth Avenue. This building, opened in 1911, houses almost half of the 10 million volumes in the collection.
Above A sidewalk Santa Claus joins admirers of the traditional Christmas displays in a smart Fifth Avenue store window.

Opposite far left The Plaza Hotel, one of the grandest of New York's hotels, opened in 1907 and retains that era's elegance.

Opposite near left The colorful Byzantine St Bartholomew's Church on Park Avenue between 50th and 51st Streets was built in 1902.

Opposite bottom: The ornate north face of the New York General Building (now owned by the Helmsley Corporation) which sits astride Park Avenue has two pedestrian passages leading from 42nd to 43rd Street, while the two tall portals allow traffic to circulate around Grand Central Station above street level.

Right The Flatiron building owes its triangular shape to its location on 23rd Street where Fifth Avenue intersects Broadway. Erected in 1902, it is one of the first New York buildings to be entirely supported on a steel frame.

Above Lever House, erected in 1952, was the first of New York's glass-encased office buildings. Rising behind is the Seagram Building.
Left above The Pierpont Morgan Library, designed by McKim, Mead and White in 1906, has a collection of early books and manuscripts.
Left Macy's, the world's largest department store, occupies an entire block, except for the corner building with its hotdog stand.

Above The General Assembly of the United Nations in session on the East River.
Below The illuminated towers of the Chrysler building are typical of the dazzling New York lights.

Above Manhattan from the East River: The UN, the Empire State and the Chrysler Buildings.

Below Paley Park, on East 53rd Street, off Fifth Avenue is a new 'pocket park.'

The magic of Broadway is epitomized by the marquees and lights of the theater district.

Broadway

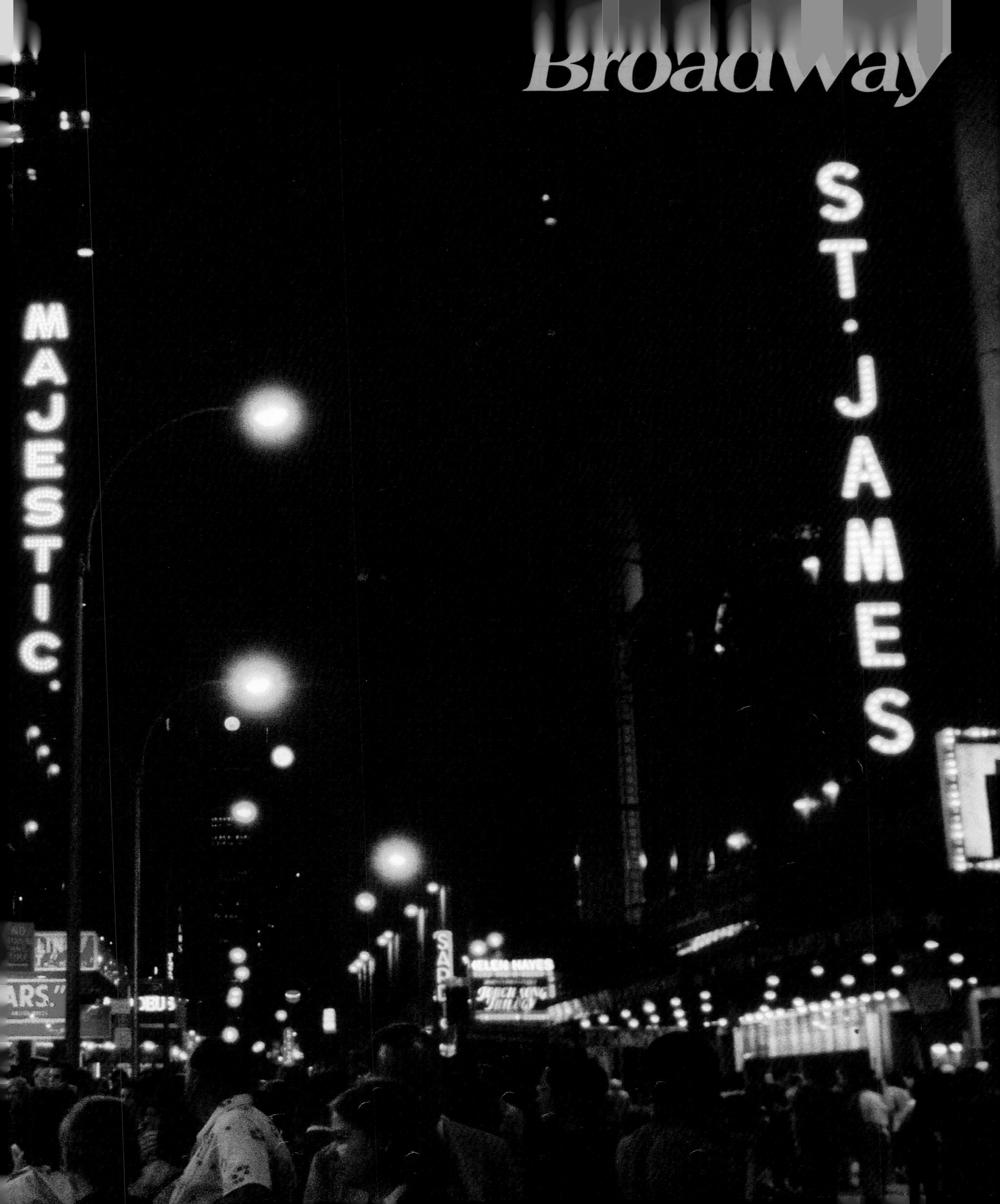

Broadway

When it began, Broadway was just that—a 'broad way' that cut northward through the center of Manhattan Island. It had actually been an Indian trail, but eventually the English colonists began to build some fine houses, churches and commercial buildings on lower Broadway. As the city moved steadily northward, so did Broadway, and as it did, the city's living patterns changed. After 1850, Broadway became almost exclusively the thoroughfare for commercial structures—stores, offices, hotels and such. Theaters, too, gravitated toward Broadway: it was central, it was accessible, it was lively. But many of the first theaters that settled on and about Broadway were not what later generations would call 'legitimate' theaters; they staged vaudeville, burlesque, and other such popular entertainments. One of the first to build in the present Broadway district was Oscar Hammerstein, who established his theater at 42nd Street and Seventh Avenue in 1892. Soon other theaters were being built in the area around Times Square (although it was not known by that name until The New York Times Company settled there in 1906). Hotels followed, for it soon became apparent that many of the people who liked to go to the theater came from out of town.

By the 1920s, so many theaters had congregated around the 42nd Street and Broadway area that this district became known as 'The Great White Way' from all the illuminated marquees. Today fewer than 20 legitimate theaters remain there, although there are many movie theaters (some showing not-so-legitimate films) that continue to keep the district in 'white light.'

And if it is fashionable to decry the decline of serious theater on Broadway—to accuse it of settling for popular entertainment and flashy musicals—it must also be admitted that Broadway remains a touchstone by which many theater people still define the best work. There is 'Off–Broadway' and there is 'Off–Off–Broadway,' and many of those productions would still like to prove their worth 'On Broadway.' Broadway has not lost its magical appeal.

Above On the streets adjoining Broadway are many of the theaters where people come to see long-running hits or new shows in tryout.
Opposite In the middle of Duffy Square, north of Times Square on Broadway, the New York Theater owners and producers have set up an office where it is possible to buy tickets at reduced prices for any seat still unsold on the day of performance.

Above The name says it all. The glow at the marquee of one of New York's best-known theaters explains why the street was called 'the Great White Way.'

Below On Broadway, even the disagreeable experience of getting a parking ticket is lessened if the policeman confronting the driver is one of the many mounted officers who patrol the streets and parks.

Above Although strictly speaking not a part of Broadway, Radio City Music Hall at Rockefeller Center seems to embody the Broadway tradition that insists 'the show must go on.' Since 1932 Radio City Music Hall has been host to about every form of theatrical production except straight plays. Once a competitor of Broadway, it is now a staunch ally in live entertainment.

Fifth Avenue and Rockefeller Center

The statue of 'Prometheus Bringing Light to the World' symbolizes the spirit John D Rockefeller Jr hoped his 'city within a city' would bring to New York during the Depression.

Fifth Avenue and Rockefeller Center

As the nineteenth century found New Yorkers pushing their residences and commercial enterprises steadily northward, the fashionable and wealthy tended to choose Fifth Avenue as their favored thoroughfare for residence. The elegant houses moved up the avenue, accompanied by handsome churches. St Patrick's Cathedral was built between 1858 and 1888. Located at Fifth Avenue between 50th and 51st Streets, many of its parishoners complained that the church was too far out in the country.

But the city soon expanded in that direction, too much so for many of the fashionable, who found that commercial establishments were constantly encroaching on Fifth Avenue. When Benjamin Altman opened his new store at 34th Street and Fifth Avenue, despite its discreet architecture, it outraged the neighbors. The avenue's claim to serious style was fixed, however, when the New York Public Library was built, between 1899 and 1911, at Fifth Avenue and 42nd Street.

But even the library and fine churches could not hold back the commercial development that gradually pushed most residents on Fifth Avenue below 14th Street or above 59th Street. The shops were smart and expensive, but they were still stores. The great transformation of Midtown Fifth Avenue into a center of civic pride and pleasure came about when John D Rockfeller, Jr decided to construct an ambitious 'city within a city' on land he leased from Columbia University. The groundbreaking began in 1931, and the last building of the formal complex known as Rockefeller Center was not completed until 1947. There are 13 buildings in all, covering some 17 acres; the architect in charge of the overall design was Wallace K Harrison, who would also play a major role in designing the UN Headquarters and Lincoln Center. Millions of people now frequent Rockefeller Center, whether for daily jobs or mere sightseeing, but all would agree that it makes Fifth Avenue and the city itself a finer and happier place.

Above To many people, the very heart of New York is the place where Fifth Avenue and 57th Street across. On these corners are found such New York institutions as Tiffany's and Bergdorf Goodman. At Christmas time the street is hung with lights.
Opposite Pedestrians walk along the west side of Fifth Avenue; despite the crowds and traffic, movement is usually quite brisk.

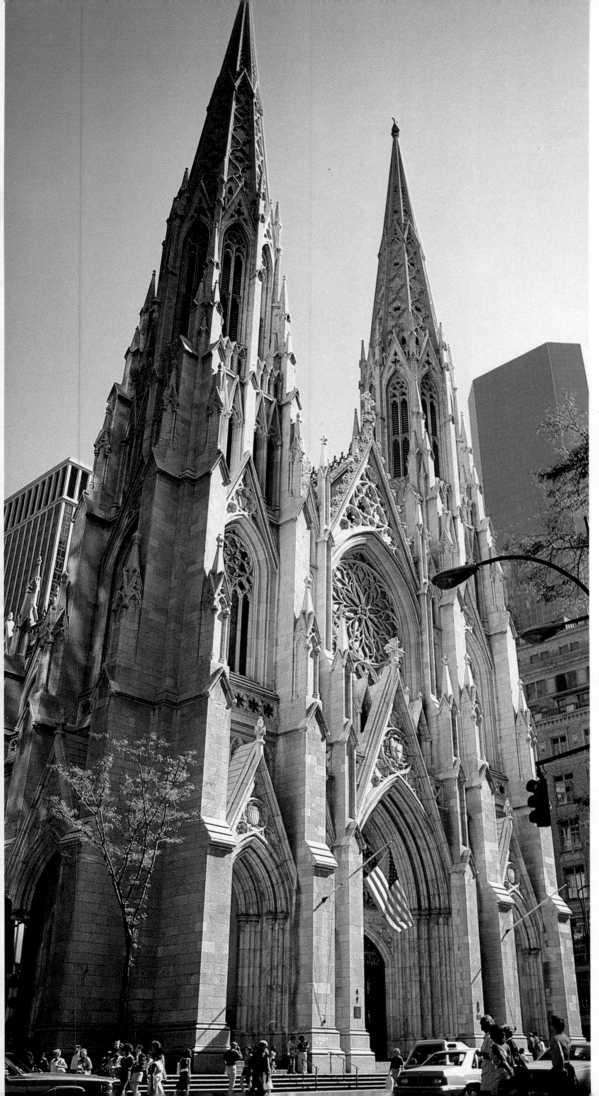

Opposite The Trump Tower is one of the many new buildings of Fifth Avenue.
Left St Patrick's, built on Fifth Avenue, between 1858 and 1888, is the cathedral of the Roman Catholic Archdiocese of New York.
Above 'Atlas Supporting the World' stands outside Rockefeller Center.
Below A traditional part of the St Patrick's Day parade up Fifth Avenue is the pipe bands.

Top At times Fifth Avenue is suprisingly devoid of crowds and traffic.
Above Pedestrians await the 'Walk' signal at a Fifth Avenue corner.
Right The glamourous interior lobby of the Trump Tower, one of the
newest and most expensive condominium-apartments on Fifth Avenue.
Opposite The annual lighting of the Christmas tree which towers over
Rockefeller Plaza is a New York tradition.

The apartment houses along Central Park West include some of the oldest buildings in this part of the city. The Dakota, which is just visible at the left was so-called because it was that far out of town.

The West Side

THE AMERICAN MVSEVM OF NATVRAL HISTORY
FOVNDED 1869

American
Museum of
Natural
History

The West Side

Some neighborhoods and sections of New York City evoke almost immediate and universal associations: Greenwich Village or Harlem, for example. But other sections leave many, even native New Yorkers, uncertain in their response. One such area is the West Side, despite the fact that millions first view New York from this perspective when they arrive via the Port Authority Bus Terminal or Penn Station. Many others spend pleasurable hours in the West Side's institutions: The Lincoln Center for the Performing Arts and the Madison Square Garden Center are only two of the region's attractions.

Not to be confused with the Upper West Side, which is mainly residential, the West Side extends from about 72nd Street at the north to about 34th Street in the south, and from Sixth Avenue on the east to the Hudson River on the west. Included in this broadly defined West Side are several distinct sections, including the Garment District and Hell's Kitchen. The former, one of the world's major suppliers and shapers of fabric, grew up in the 1920s, when garment manufacturers moved here from the Lower East Side. Hell's Kitchen, the neighborhood from the 20s through the 50s west of Eighth Avenue, has been home base for impoverished immigrants—originally Irish, later Italians and Greeks, now mainly Hispanics.

The West Side that is most frequented today, though, is a more restricted section, and that is the territory that provides a home for some of the world's greatest cultural and educational institutions: the Metropolitan Opera, New York City Ballet, the New York Philharmonic, Juilliard School of Music, and the American Museum of Natural History, to name but the best known. And when the Madison Square Garden Center and the New York Coliseum are joined soon by the new Convention Center, then indeed the West Side can claim to be one of New York's most popular sections. The hub of America's classical performing arts and a multi-ethnic neighborhood, the West Side reflects the diversity characteristic of all of New York City.

Above The Avenue of the Americas—or Sixth Avenue, as it continues to be called by most New Yorkers—is a lively West Side thoroughfare.
Left The original building of the American Museum of Natural History, constructed between 1874-77 in the Romanesque Revival style faces the New York Historical Society on West 77th Street.

Opposite top An evening view of the Lincoln Center for the Performing Arts looking past the fountain in the central Plaza to the Metropolitan Opera House. Lincoln Center was first discussed in 1955, and John D Rockefeller III was among those instrumental in getting the project underway. It meant dislocating hundreds of residents, but it brought a great deal of new money into this deteriorating section of the city and has proven to be a magnet for the redevelopment of this whole part of the West Side. Lincoln Center also includes such buildings as Avery Fisher Hall, home to the New York Philharmonic Orchestra, the New York State Theater, home to the New York City Opera and the New York City Ballet, as well as the Julliard School of Music, the Vivian Beaumont Theater and the Library of the Performing Arts.

Opposite bottom Carnegie Hall remains New York's premier concert hall. Erected in 1891, it was threatened with destruction in the 1960s, but musicians and others rallied to save it. In addition to its historical associations and superb acoustics, Carnegie has a labyrinth of studios and practice rooms.

Above Looking down on the interior lobby of the Metropolitain Opera House. Many decorative elements were presented by foreign governments as a tribute to the international harmony fostered by opera.

Right The New York Coliseum at Columbus Circle provides vast spaces necessary for exhibitions and trade shows.

Above One of the most restful yet stimulating locales in New York is the sculpture garden of The Museum of Modern Art (Usually referred to as 'The Modern' or simply MOMA). The original building on this site was opened in 1939; additions have enlarged it considerably since, but its sculpture garden—designed by the architect Philip Johnson—has retained its original atmosphere. Superb examples of modern sculpture—by masters such as Rodin, Renoir, Maillol, Moore and Picasso—can be viewed at leisure and in a setting that allows them to be studied from all angles.

Left The main entrance to the American Museum of Natural History is on Central Park West. Sometimes known as the Roosevelt Wing, it celebrates the exploits of Theodore Roosevelt, who was a writer, naturalist and early conservationist, as well as being a consummate politician and the 26th President of the United States. Within the museum are found massive collections of American Indian artifacts, gems and minerals dinosaur skeletons, animal dioramas, and the world-famous Hayden Planaterium.

Opposite: One of the great sights of the Macy's Thanksgiving Day Parade is the number of giant balloons of well-known cartoon characters.

Central Park
and Environs

Central Park and Environs

Most of the world's great cities take pleasure in some large park in their midst, but none takes more pleasure and pride than does New York in its Central Park. The foresight of New York's citizens to set aside this relatively large piece of valuable land has been fulfilled and rewarded many times over. Since 1965, Central Park has even been designated a National Historic Landmark, but even if most New Yorkers or visitors don't know this for a fact, they know a national treasure when they see it.

The story of how Central Park was set aside has been told many times but can never be repeated too often. As early as in 1844, the poet and journalist William Cullen Bryant was suggesting that the city set aside just such a public park; by 1850, the idea had spread so that both candidates for mayor were promising to work for this project: this was one campaign promise that was well kept. The land selected was at that time well out of town and was described as 'A pestilential spot where miasmic odors taint every breath of air,' but by 1856 some 840 acres were acquired, swamps were drained, and the pigs and bone—boiling factory there were dispossessed.

A competition was held for the park's design, and of the 33 designs submitted, the winner was the one called 'Greensward,' by Frederick Law Olmstead and Calvert Vaux. The park that so many people still enjoy remains quite true to their design—including the then—revolutionary sunken transverse roads—but the desire to keep the park relatively 'natural' has often conflicted with the desire to make full use of its environment. Thus, in addition to boating on the lake, horse—back riding on the paths, occasional bicycle and foot races on the roads, jogging on the trails, amateur sporting events on the fields and free concerts on the meadows, there are tennis courts and two iceskating rinks, a zoo and a bandshell, a theater for 'Shakespeare in the Park' and a restaurant—not to mention the Metropolitan Museum of Art. But the guardians of Central Park's unique values remain vigilant, and the Park will undoubtedly go on giving pleasure and pride to generations to come.

Previous spread A popular summer pastime is sailing radio-controlled yachts on the boat pond in Central Park.
Opposite Iceskaters at the Wollman Memorial Rink in Central Park.
Above The Tavern on the Green, built on the site of a late-nineteenth century sheepfold near 67th Street and Central Park West, is now an elegant and expensive restaurant, with dancing.

FINISH NEW YORK CITY FINISH

Opposite far left The Bethesda Fountain on the Terrace at the south side of the lake where it is possible to rent rowboats. Beyond the roadway can be seen the Goldman Band Shell.
Above Central Park's interior roadways are used for various sporting events such as this long-distance bicycle race; countless amateur bicyclists also ride through the Park, especially on weekends when the roads are closed to vehicular traffic.
Left A group of musicians offers a free jazz concert, one of the many spontaneous events in the Park.
Below One of the best-known competitions to have grown up in New York in recent years is the New York City Marathon. The route of 26 miles winds through all five boroughs and finishes in Central Park.
Right above Another recent phenomenon is the number of specialized food vendors who tend to concentrate along the edges of Central Park.
Right below Many of the second-hand book-stores sell stock from portable stalls on the southeastern corner of Central Park.

Right A street entertainer performs in Grand Army Plaza, the refreshing square on the Fifth Avenue corner of Central Park.

Right middle The central portico, or main entrance, of the Metropolitan Museum of Art, which extends along the edge of Central Park on Fifth Avenue between 80th and 84th Streets. This portion of the museum was designed by Richard Morris Hunt and built between 1895 and 1902. The Metropolitan ranks as one of the world's greatest art museums.

Opposite far right top The General Motors Building on Fifth Avenue, opposite the Plaza Hotel created some controversy when built in 1968, because it introduced an automobile showroom beside the elegant Fifth Avenue shops.

Opposite far right bottom The Museum of the City of New York has occupied this building on upper Fifth Avenue since 1932. Its collections and displays capture the history and spirit of New York City.

Right middle bottom The Guggenheim Museum, on Fifth Avenue between 88th and 89th Streets, was designed by Frank Lloyd Wright, and built in 1959, the last work he supervised. It has a distinguished collection of twentieth century art, but is equally admired for its use of central space and the spiral ramp.

Below Temple Emanu-El on the corner of 65th Street and Fifth Avenue, once the site of Mrs Astor's mansion, seats 2500 worshippers, more than St Patrick's.

The George Washington Bridge was opened in 1931 (with a lower level added in 1962); a work of beauty, it carries over 50 million vehicles a year between New York and New Jersey. The views are outstanding.

Upper East Side and Above The Park

In a city known for diversity, perhaps no place demonstrates the sharp contrasts more dramatically than East 96th Street, which extends from Central Park at Fifth Avenue all the way to the East River. The south side of 96th Street belongs to one of the most chic and expensive sections of New York City, and thus of the world: The Upper East Side. Yet directly across 96th Street, on its north side, is East, or Spanish Harlem, a section of great vitality but hardly chic or expensive.

The Upper East Side extends from 96th Street down into the 50s, and from Fifth Avenue to the East River, but in recent years it has come to designate more a style of life than a geographic locale. It was not always so, although the seeds were planted in the early decades of the nineteenth century when wealthy people began to build their fine homes along Fifth and Madison Avenues. Not until after World War I, when the railroad tracks and yards that connected to Grand Central Station were moved underground did the whole East Side be come desirable to the fashionable. Some old neighborhoods would survive—Yorkville, long a center of German immigrants, is perhaps the most notable—and by no means is every block of the Upper East Side as prosperous or chic as the next. But since World War II, the Upper East Side has definitely attracted people of considerable wealth. Fine restaurants, smart boutiques, embassies, art galleries—these distinguish the Upper East Side today.

The vast area of upper Manhattan—above 96th Street on the east side, above Central Park and 110th Street elsewhere—could hardly be summed up in such few words. In addition to East Harlem—now dominated by Puerto Ricans—there is the traditional Harlem: although the blacks began to move up there in the early years of the century, it was not until the 1920s that the great influx began and Harlem became a world of its own. Upper Manhattan also includes Morningside Heights, dominated by Columbia University; Washington Heights, apartments and the Columbia–Presbyterian Medical Center; and the northern tip of Manhattan, overlooked by The Cloisters. Each is a special realm, but all together make up Manhattan.

Left This splash of color on a balcony in Harlem highlights the adaptability of this legendary community's inhabitants.
Above A tramway car at the Manhattan station (Second Avenue and 59th Street) of the tramway that connects Manhattan to Roosevelt Island in the middle of the East River. Formerly Welfare Island, it now has apartment houses for low and middle income residents.

Above The granite and marble mausoleum, Grant's Tomb, was dedicated in 1897, the 75th anniversary of President Ulysses S Grant's birth. The pediment is inscribed with Grant's words, 'Let us have Peace.' Grant's wife is buried beside him. The memorial was paid by public subscription, a testimony to America's high regard for Grant.

Left The Cloisters, the unique collection of medieval art and architecture at Fort Tryon Park, high above the Hudson River, is a branch of the Metropolitan Museum of Art. An amalgam of actual elements of medieval monasteries from all over Europe, it houses superb works of early Christian art, such as triptychs and sculpture.

Above A view into the bakery window of Bloomingdale's, the epitome of Upper East Side style.

Right Gracie Mansion. The official residence of the Mayor of New York, stands in Carl Schutz Park, opposite 88th Street, on the East River. Begun in 1770, it was rebuilt in 1798 by Archibald Gracie, whose name it still bears.

Below The Morris-Jumel Mansion, at 160th Street and Edgecombe Avenue, was built by Roger Morris in 1765. Washington made it his headquarters in 1776, and planned the Battle of Haarlem Heights here. Stephen Jumel, a rich French merchant, bought the house in 1810. Its period rooms are breathtaking.

Above Avery Hall at Columbia University was designed by McKim, Mead and White in 1912; it houses the school of architecture.

Right The interior of the Cathedral Church of St John the Divine; the largest church built in modern times, it is still under construction.

The Soldiers' and Sailors' Memorial Arch forms the centerpiece of the Grand Army Plaza at the entrance to Prospect Park in Brooklyn.

The Other Boroughs

THE DEFENDERS OF THE UNION 1861 1865

The Other Boroughs

It is open to debate whether Manhattanites or out–of–towners need more to be reminded that New York City is not confined to Manhattan Island. Indeed, New York City is composed of five boroughs and has been ever since 1898. Each of the boroughs has enjoyed its own history and has developed its own look and feel over the years.

There is Brooklyn, for one. With its population of some 2,600,000 it would rate by itself as the fourth largest city in the United States. Founded by the Dutch in 1636, Brooklyn developed first as a rural area, then as a residential area, and with its growing harbor works eventually attracted considerable light industry. Once the home of Walt Whitman and now home to many blacks and Italian–Americans as well as to other ethnic groups—including the middle class who have recently been 'gentrifying' certain neighborhoods—Brooklyn remains a distinctive city–within–a–city.

The next best known of the other boroughs is the Bronx—if for no other reason that the Yankees, New York's premier sports team, are based here and have become known as The Bronx Bombers, or that millions of people have enjoyed the Bronx Zoo. The Bronx was also settled first by the Dutch, but got its name from an early landowner, a Dane, Jonas Bronck. The Bronx is characterized by extensive apartment houses and green stretches, and is the only one of the five boroughs that is entirely on the mainland.

Queens is the largest of the boroughs—with some 155 square miles—and although there is some industry within it, Queens remains essentially a collection of residential neighborhoods. Not many of its inhabitants know that it was named after Queen Catherine, wife of Charles II, but they hardly ever need to be reminded that it is the home of both LaGuardia and Kennedy International Airports.

And finally there is Staten Island—correctly the borough of Richmond—long almost a rural–pastoral stepchild of New York City, but since its direct linkage with Brooklyn in 1964 via the Verrazano–Narrows Bridge, increasingly more populated and developed.

Left The Japanese Garden, one section of the Brooklyn Botanic Garden behind the Brooklyn Museum. Laid out in 1915, the garden includes examples of traditional Japanese plants and gardening styles.
Above A section of the famed amusement park at Coney Island, with its Wonder Wheel; although the rides and attractions have decreased in recent years, many people still come here with a sense of nostalgia.

Above One of the two great arches of the Brooklyn Bridge, joining Manhattan and Brooklyn. The opening of this bridge in 1883, heralded as the 'eighth wonder of the world,' brought Brooklyn into the mainstream of New York life.

Left Typical row houses in Brooklyn which after many years of decline are being lovingly restored by younger owners who cherish the old fashioned neighborhoods of the other boroughs.

Below A section of Swan Lake, in Brooklyn's Prospect Park, which was designed by Frederick Law Olmstead, of Central Park fame.

Yankee Stadium, the home of the Yankees baseball team in the Bronx, is also used for many other events including large religious assemblies. Built in 1923, in the heyday of Babe Ruth's fabulous career, it has a short right field.

The control tower and International Arrivals
Building at Kennedy Airport in Queens.

Above The Bronx Zoo, located on over 250 acres laid out in 1899, is the largest zoo in the United States. Over 100 species live here; many like these deer, roam in natural environments.
Right The Verrazano-Narrows Bridge rises above Fort Hamilton, which once guarded the harbor on the Brooklyn side. Across the Narrows on Staten Island is Fort Wadsworth.
Below Horse racing can be seen at Aqueduct Race Track, in Queens.

A street performer's juggling act entrances the delighted crowd gathered on the steps of the Metropolitain Museum of Art.

The People You See

The People You See

New York City is spectacular buildings and the theater and communications and finance and corporate headquarters and sports teams, but above all, New York City is people. Some 7,500,000 of them, and a more diverse and individualistic lot of people than probably in any other such large city in the world.

Long before the United Nations settled in New York, the city had served as a magnet for peoples from all over the world. The Dutch and English came first—always excepting the Indians—but soon came other groups such as the Germans. The great waves of immigrants, however, did not begin until the mid–nineteenth century: first the Irish, the Italians, and then by the turn of the century the Jews. After World War I, American blacks moved up to New York in large numbers, while after World War II came a great influx of Puerto Ricans. Meanwhile there had been many smaller but still significant groups—Chinese, Hungarians, Ukrainians, Poles, Armenians, and Greeks, just to name some—and in more recent years there have come such new groups as Cubans, Haitians, Filipinos, Russians.

The result is a city that is now almost 25 percent black, 20 percent Hispanic, about 15 percent Italian, 10 percent Irish and 20 percent Jewish. Many of these peoples keep alive their own traditional ways—foods, music, dance, holidays, traditions, and general lifestyles—whether within the privacy of their own families or on the streets of New York, and this gives rise to the extraordinary color and diversity of life throughout the city.

Perhaps because they must live constantly surrounded by competing demands on their senses and sensibilities, New Yorkers sometimes strike out–of–towners as a bit blasé or even callous. But just as people who live in the countryside cannot exclaim over every gorgeous tree or animal, New Yorkers must put many things into the background to go about their daily lives. Street-smart but receptive to the cultural wealth surrounding them, New Yorkers themselves are the lifeblood of the city.

Left One of many small, impromptu 'farmer's markets' that spring up on vacant lots around New York. They sell vegetables, fruits and flowers to New Yorkers and tourists.
Above New Yorkers are always ready to try some food, ordinary or unconventional, at an outdoor stand. The Italian festival of San Gennaro is famed for its hot sausage.

bove A group of musicians give an *al fresco* concert on a corner of Washington Square ark. Many musicians, from classical olinists to folksingers to jazz saxophonists, n be heard on the sidewalks and parks of ew York. Some play to earn money, while hers, like this group, play for their own easure.

pposite top Some of 'New York's Finest' ke a break. The New York Police epartment, although reduced in numbers, mains the nation's largest, and women form increasingly large percentage of the force.

pposite far left A New York City fireman uses in his exertions by a firetruck. Many eman have lost their lives in the city's rvice. There is a moving memorial to these ave men and women in St John the Divine.

pposite near left The diversity of nationalities New York is evident on every street. though some groups readily assimilate, hers retain and display their distinct entities in custom as in dress.

ight Two weary shoppers rest in front of the fth Avenue windows of B Altman's, one of fth Avenue's department stores. With the test in fashion, fads and foods, and the nsity of its stores, the city is a favorite for ew York and suburban shoppers.

verleaf A man hurries along the esplanade in ooklyn Heights in the rain. The skyline of wer Manhattan forms a somber but still pressive backdrop on this grey day.